GRATITUDE JOURNAL for TEEN GIRLS

Copyright © 2023 by Dazzling Prints Publishing
All rights reserved. This book or any portion thereof may not be reproduced or used in any manner whatsoever without the express written permission of the publisher except for the use of brief quotations in a book review.

This gratitude
journal belongs to:

_____

_____

10 POSITIVE QUOTES OF GRATITUDE TO LIVE BY

- Choose to Be Grateful
- There is JOY in the Journey!
- Be Grateful
- Give Thanks for a Little and You will Find a Lot
- I AM Thankful!
- I AM Grateful to Be Alive!
- I AM Blessed!
- I'll have an attitude of Gratitude
- Choose Joy!
- Im Thankful for all that I Have

gratitude CHANGES every thing

How to Use This Journal

Hello and welcome to the Gratitude Journal for Teen Girls. This journal features reflective prompts that you can use on a daily basis to check-in with yourself, write down your feelings and practice gratitude.

We hope that you enjoy using this journal and that it helps you focus on all of the great things that you have going on in your life.

Enjoy!

Date: _____

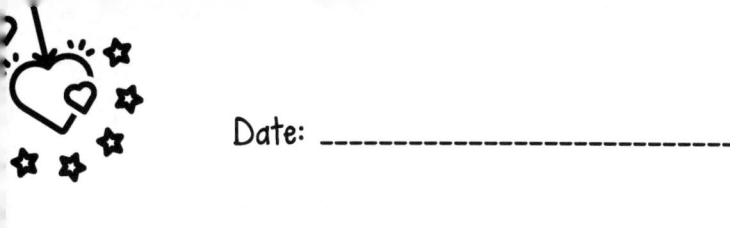

Today I Am Feeling:

_____

Today I Am Grateful For:

_____
_____
_____

Quote of the Day

3 Amazing Things That Happened Today

1. _____
2. _____
3. _____

My Happiness Scale Today:

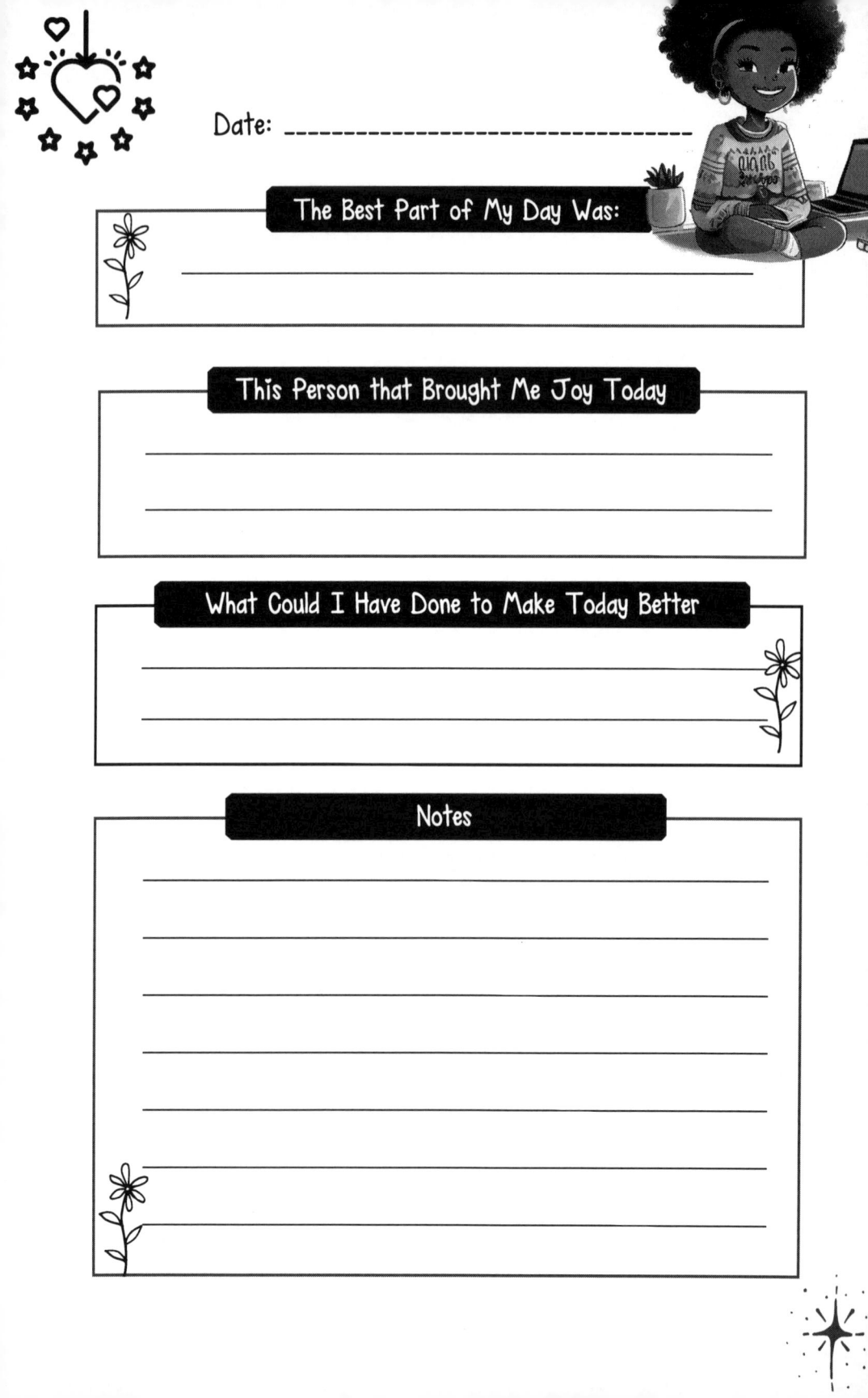

Date: _____

The Best Part of My Day Was:
_____

This Person that Brought Me Joy Today
_____
_____

What Could I Have Done to Make Today Better
_____
_____

Notes
_____
_____
_____
_____
_____
_____

Date: _____

Today I Am Feeling:

_____

Today I Am Grateful For:

_____

_____

_____

Quote of the Day

3 Amazing Things That Happened Today

1. _____
2. _____
3. _____

My Happiness Scale Today:

Date: _____

The Best Part of My Day Was:
_____

This Person that Brought Me Joy Today
_____
_____

What Could I Have Done to Make Today Better
_____
_____

Notes
_____
_____
_____
_____
_____
_____

Date: _____

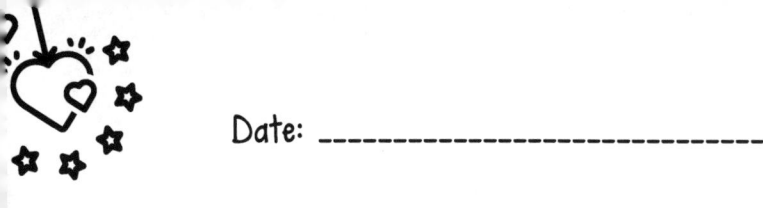

Today I Am Feeling:

_____

Today I Am Grateful For:

_____

_____

_____

Quote of the Day

3 Amazing Things That Happened Today

1. _____
2. _____
3. _____

My Happiness Scale Today:

Date: _____

The Best Part of My Day Was:
_____
_____

This Person that Brought Me Joy Today
_____
_____
_____

What Could I Have Done to Make Today Better
_____
_____
_____

Notes
_____
_____
_____
_____
_____
_____
_____

Date: _____

Today I Am Feeling:

_____

Today I Am Grateful For:

_____

_____

_____

Quote of the Day

3 Amazing Things That Happened Today

1. _____
2. _____
3. _____

My Happiness Scale Today:

Date: _____

The Best Part of My Day Was:
_____

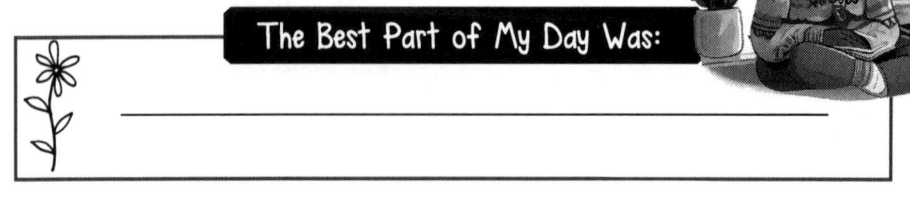

This Person that Brought Me Joy Today
_____
_____

What Could I Have Done to Make Today Better
_____
_____

Notes
_____
_____
_____
_____
_____
_____

Date: _____

Today I Am Feeling:

_____

Today I Am Grateful For:

_____
_____
_____

Quote of the Day

3 Amazing Things That Happened Today

1. _____
2. _____
3. _____

My Happiness Scale Today:

Date: _____

The Best Part of My Day Was:
_____

This Person that Brought Me Joy Today
_____
_____

What Could I Have Done to Make Today Better
_____
_____

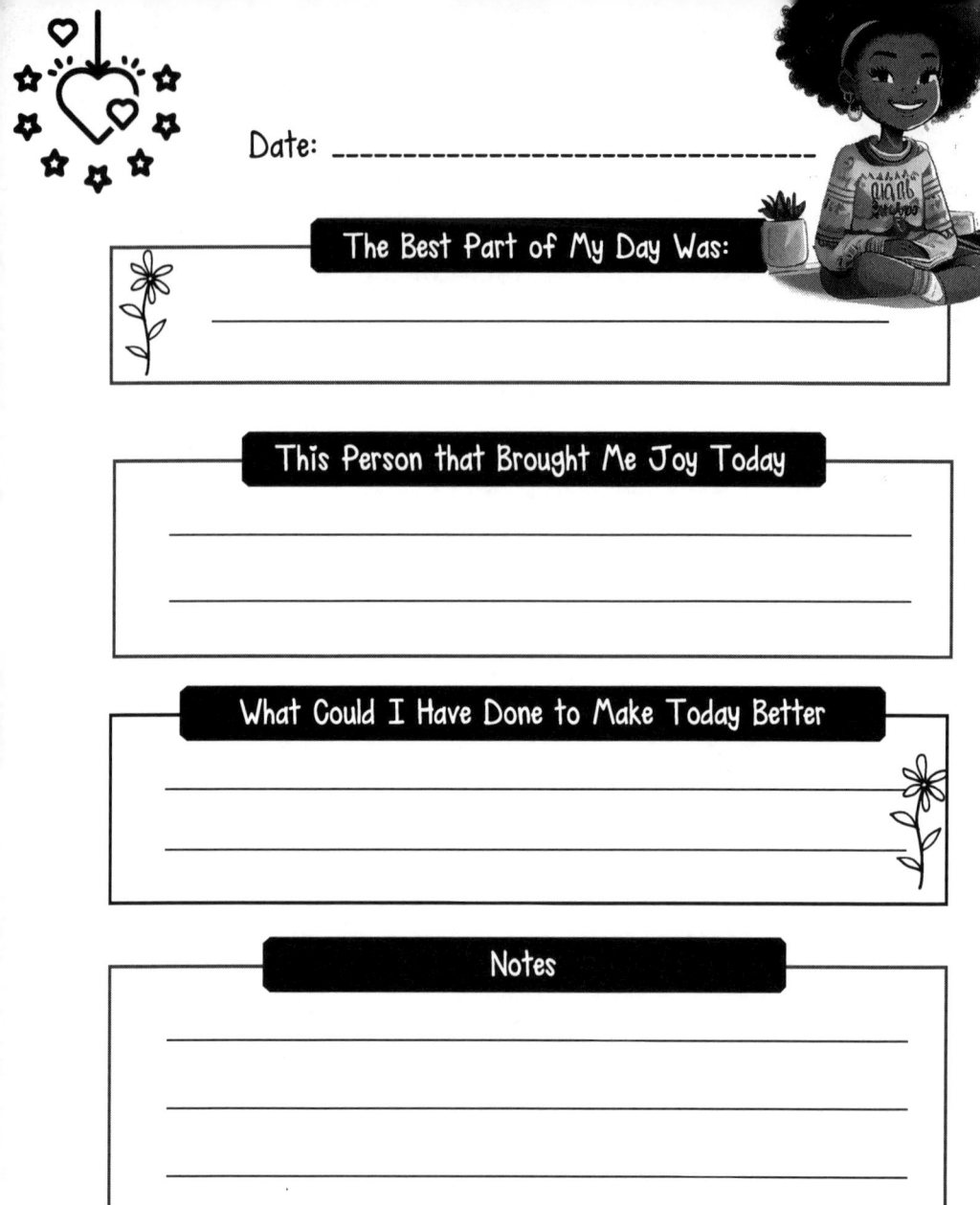

Notes
_____
_____
_____
_____
_____
_____

choose joy

Date: _____

Today I Am Feeling:

_____

Today I Am Grateful For:

_____
_____
_____

Quote of the Day

3 Amazing Things That Happened Today

1. _____
2. _____
3. _____

My Happiness Scale Today:

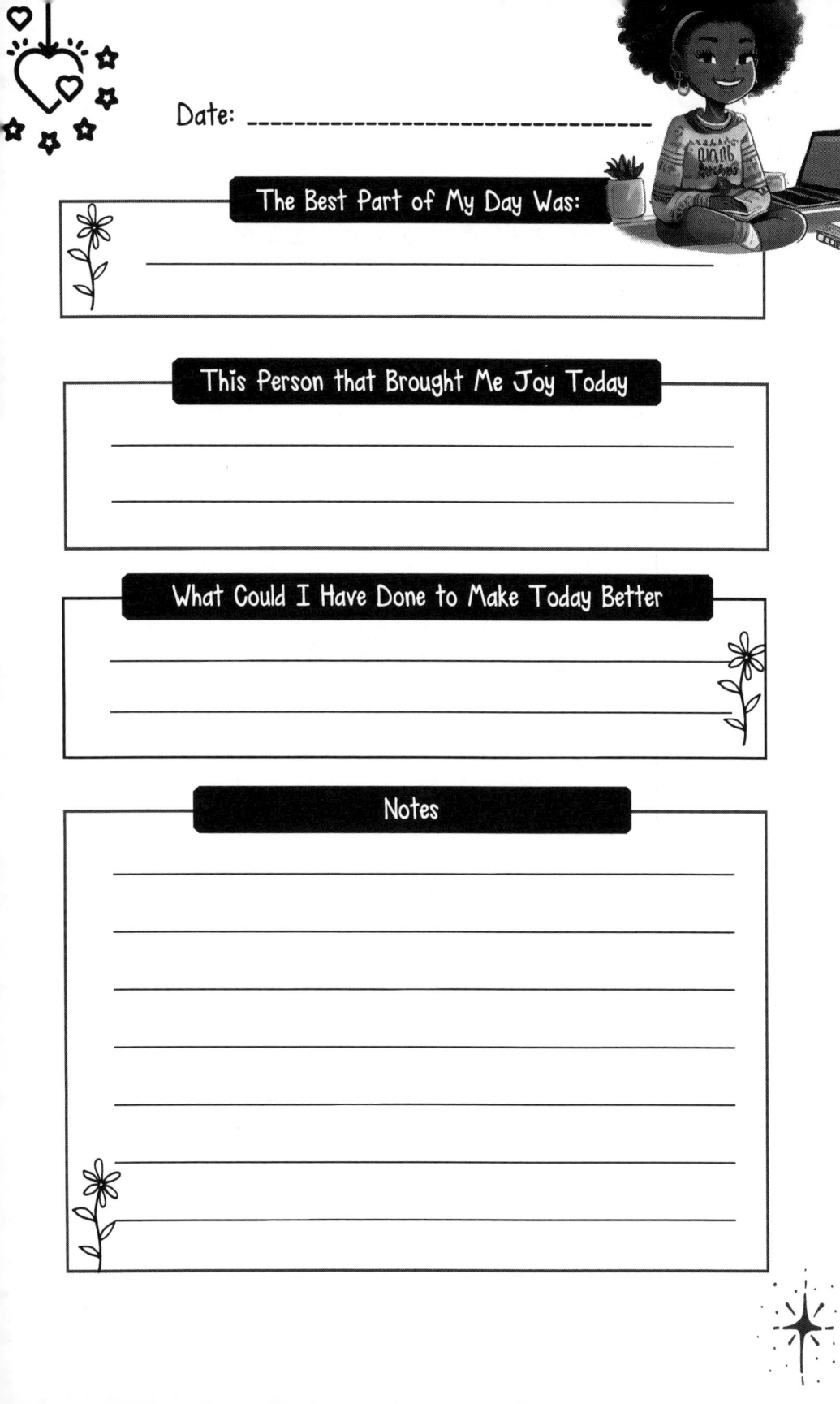

Date: _____

The Best Part of My Day Was:

_____

This Person that Brought Me Joy Today

_____
_____

What Could I Have Done to Make Today Better

_____
_____

Notes

_____
_____
_____
_____
_____
_____
_____

Date: _____

Today I Am Feeling:

_____

Today I Am Grateful For:

_____
_____
_____

Quote of the Day

3 Amazing Things That Happened Today

1. _____
2. _____
3. _____

My Happiness Scale Today:

Date: _____

The Best Part of My Day Was:

This Person that Brought Me Joy Today

What Could I Have Done to Make Today Better

Notes

Date: _____

Today I Am Feeling:
_____

Today I Am Grateful For:
_____
_____
_____

Quote of the Day

3 Amazing Things That Happened Today
1. _____
2. _____
3. _____

My Happiness Scale Today:

Date: _____

The Best Part of My Day Was:

_____

This Person that Brought Me Joy Today

_____
_____

What Could I Have Done to Make Today Better

_____
_____

Notes

_____
_____
_____
_____
_____
_____
_____

Date: _____

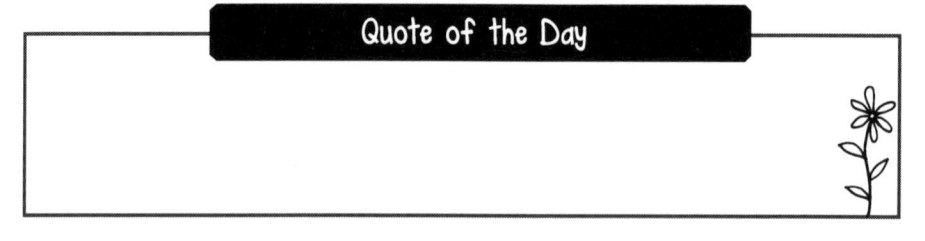

Today I Am Feeling:

_____

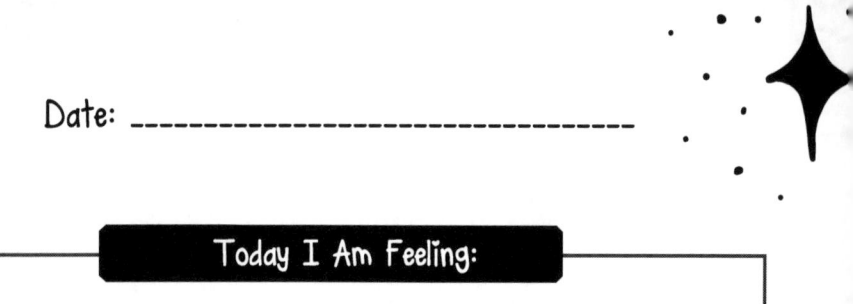

Today I Am Grateful For:

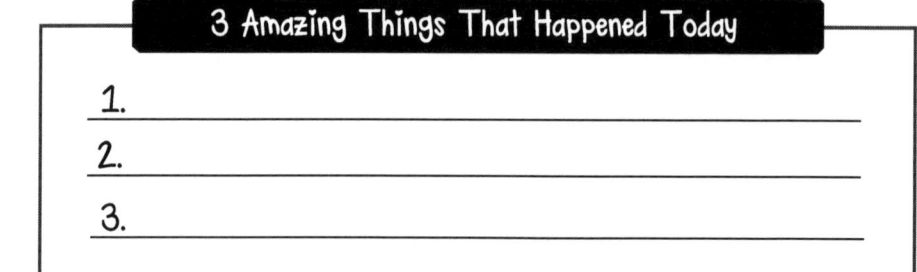

_____

_____

_____

Quote of the Day

3 Amazing Things That Happened Today

1. _____
2. _____
3. _____

My Happiness Scale Today:

Date: _____

The Best Part of My Day Was:

_____

This Person that Brought Me Joy Today

_____
_____

What Could I Have Done to Make Today Better

_____
_____

Notes

_____
_____
_____
_____
_____
_____
_____

Date: _____

Today I Am Feeling:

_____

Today I Am Grateful For:

_____
_____
_____

Quote of the Day

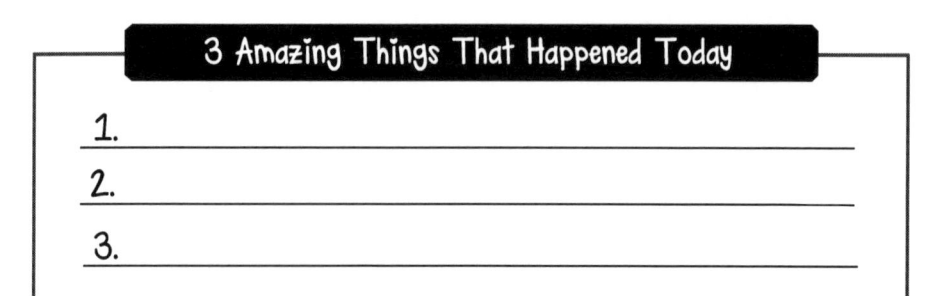

3 Amazing Things That Happened Today

1. _____
2. _____
3. _____

My Happiness Scale Today:

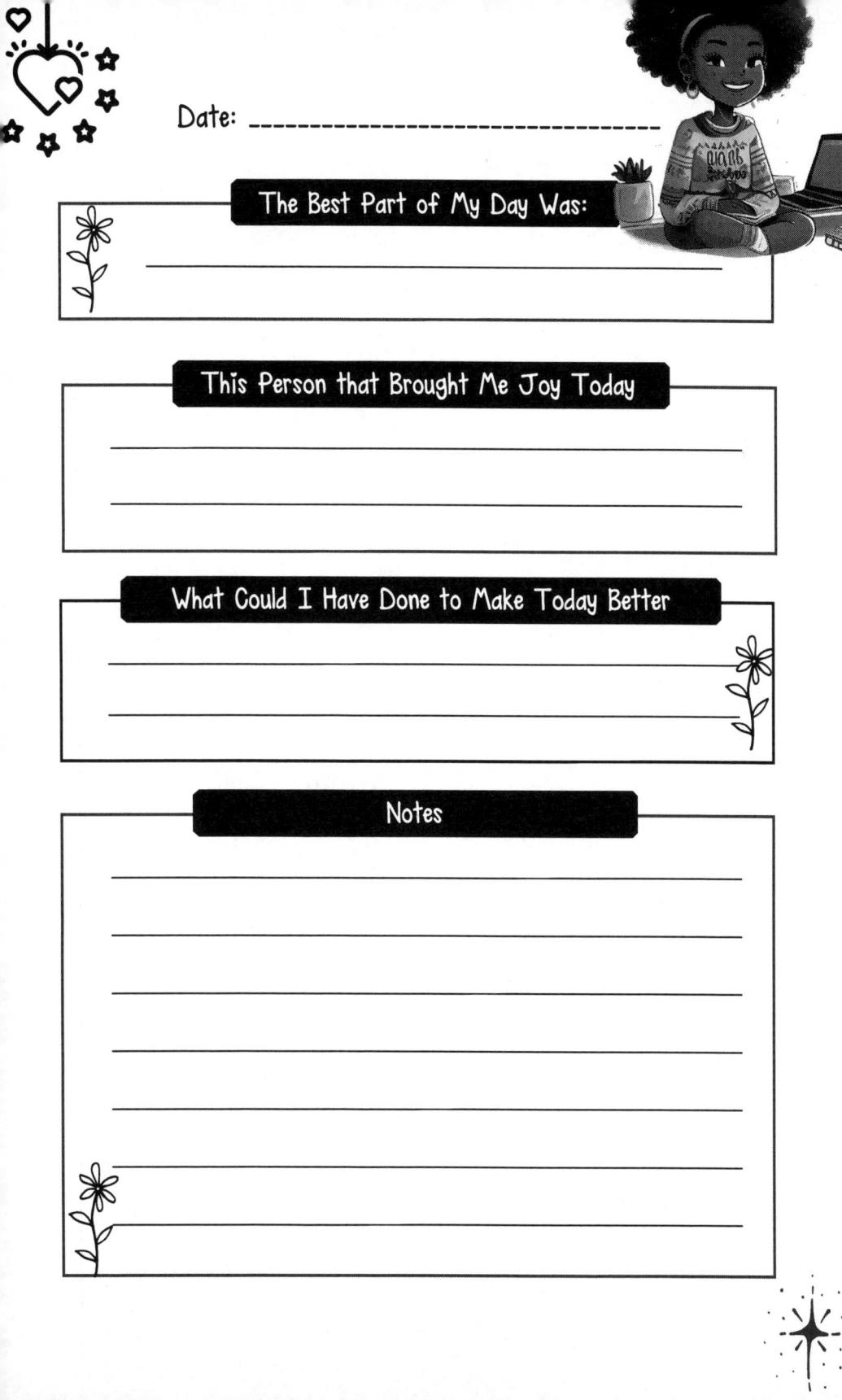

Date: _____

The Best Part of My Day Was:
_____

This Person that Brought Me Joy Today
_____
_____

What Could I Have Done to Make Today Better
_____
_____

Notes
_____
_____
_____
_____
_____
_____
_____

Date: _____

Today I Am Feeling:

_____

Today I Am Grateful For:

_____

_____

_____

Quote of the Day

3 Amazing Things That Happened Today

1. _____
2. _____
3. _____

My Happiness Scale Today:

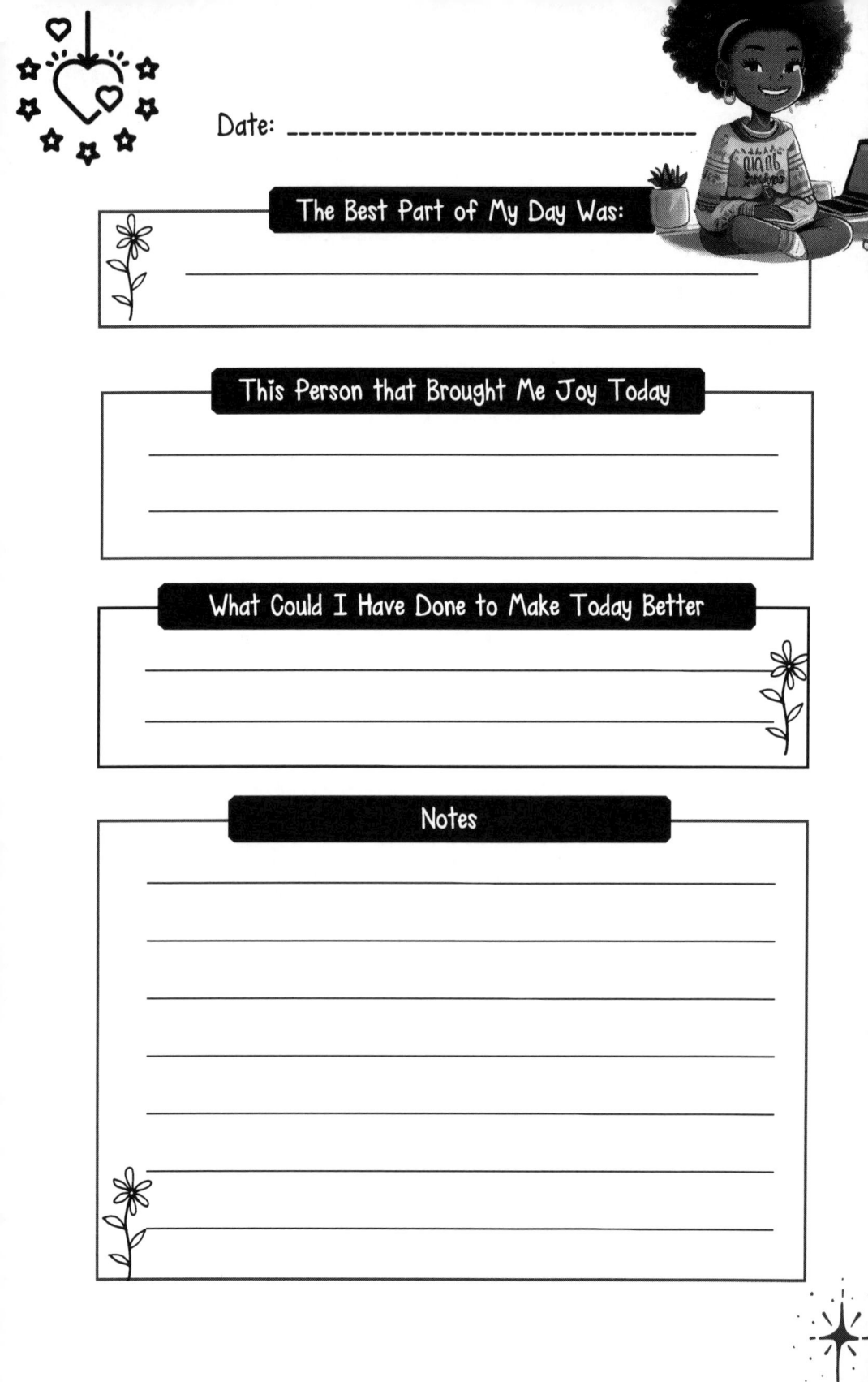

Date: _____

The Best Part of My Day Was:
_____
_____

This Person that Brought Me Joy Today
_____
_____

What Could I Have Done to Make Today Better
_____
_____

Notes
_____
_____
_____
_____
_____
_____

Date: _____

Today I Am Feeling:

_____

Today I Am Grateful For:

_____

_____

_____

Quote of the Day

3 Amazing Things That Happened Today

1. _____
2. _____
3. _____

My Happiness Scale Today:

Date: _____

The Best Part of My Day Was:
_____

This Person that Brought Me Joy Today
_____
_____

What Could I Have Done to Make Today Better
_____
_____

Notes
_____
_____
_____
_____
_____
_____
_____

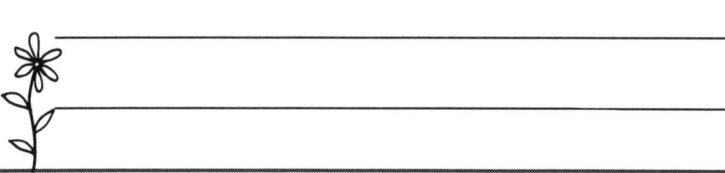

Date: _____

Today I Am Feeling:

_____

Today I Am Grateful For:

_____

_____

_____

Quote of the Day

3 Amazing Things That Happened Today

1. _____
2. _____
3. _____

My Happiness Scale Today:

Date: _____

The Best Part of My Day Was:
_____

This Person that Brought Me Joy Today
_____
_____

What Could I Have Done to Make Today Better
_____
_____

Notes
_____
_____
_____
_____
_____
_____

Date: _____

Today I Am Feeling:

_____

Today I Am Grateful For:

_____

_____

_____

Quote of the Day

3 Amazing Things That Happened Today

1. _____
2. _____
3. _____

My Happiness Scale Today:

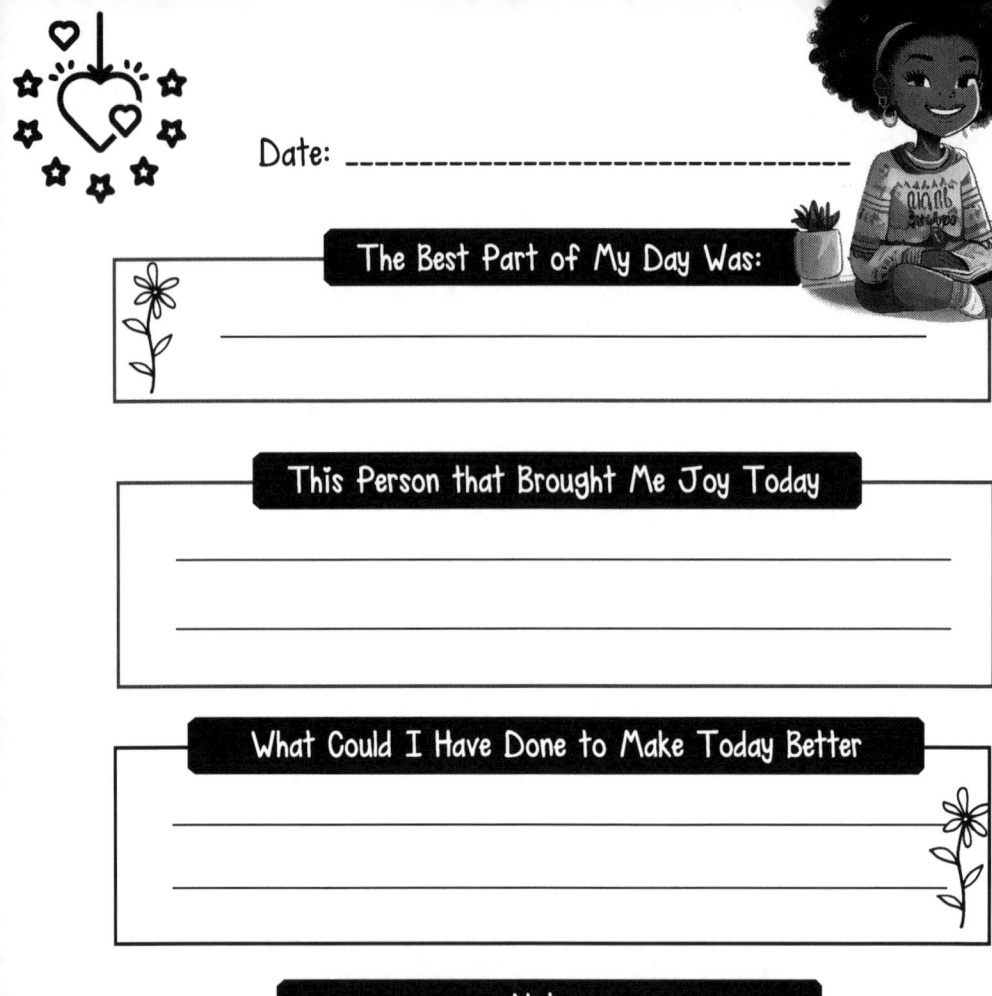

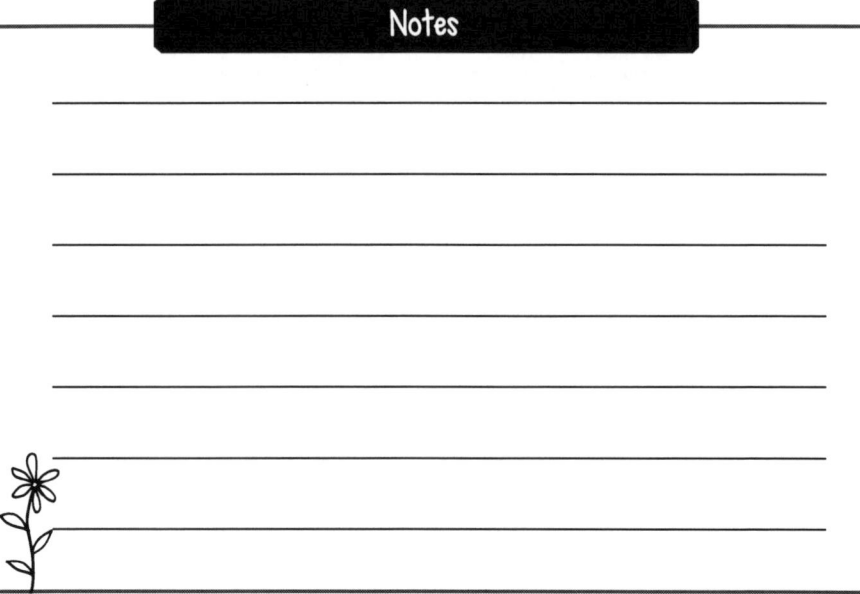

Date: _____

The Best Part of My Day Was:
_____

This Person that Brought Me Joy Today
_____
_____

What Could I Have Done to Make Today Better
_____
_____

Notes
_____
_____
_____
_____
_____
_____

Date: _____

Today I Am Feeling:
_____

Today I Am Grateful For:
_____
_____
_____

Quote of the Day

3 Amazing Things That Happened Today
1. _____
2. _____
3. _____

My Happiness Scale Today:

Date: _____

The Best Part of My Day Was:

This Person that Brought Me Joy Today

What Could I Have Done to Make Today Better

Notes

Give Thanks

Date: _____

Today I Am Feeling:

_____

Today I Am Grateful For:

_____
_____
_____

Quote of the Day

3 Amazing Things That Happened Today

1. _____
2. _____
3. _____

My Happiness Scale Today:

Date: _____

The Best Part of My Day Was:

_____

This Person that Brought Me Joy Today

_____
_____

What Could I Have Done to Make Today Better

_____
_____

Notes

_____
_____
_____
_____
_____
_____
_____

Date: _____

Today I Am Feeling:

_____

Today I Am Grateful For:

_____
_____
_____

Quote of the Day

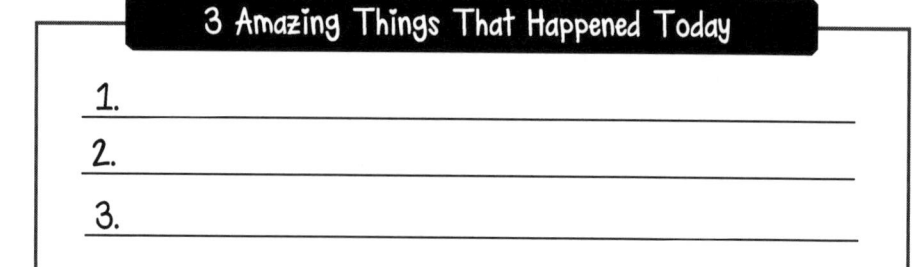

3 Amazing Things That Happened Today

1. _____
2. _____
3. _____

My Happiness Scale Today:

Date: _____

The Best Part of My Day Was:

This Person that Brought Me Joy Today

What Could I Have Done to Make Today Better

Notes

Date: _____

Today I Am Feeling:

_____

Today I Am Grateful For:

_____
_____
_____

Quote of the Day

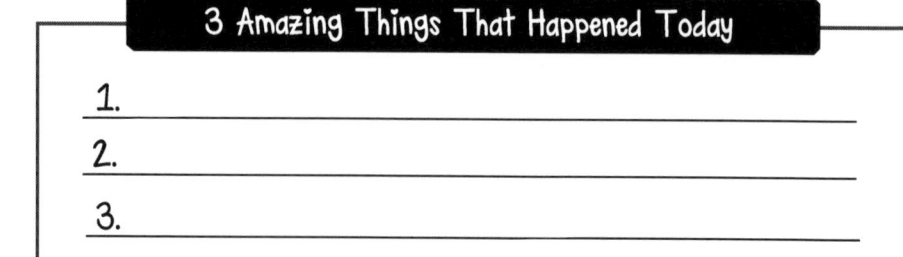

3 Amazing Things That Happened Today

1. _____
2. _____
3. _____

My Happiness Scale Today:

Date: _____

The Best Part of My Day Was:

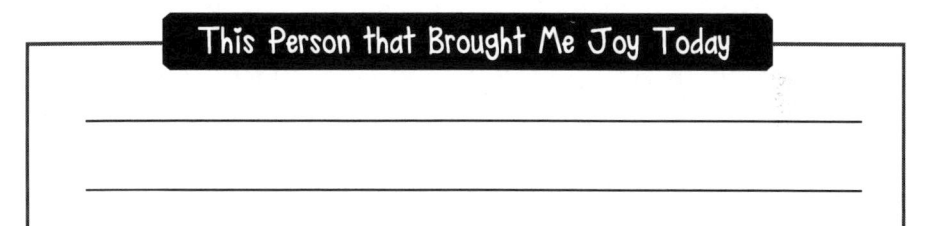

_____

This Person that Brought Me Joy Today

_____

_____

What Could I Have Done to Make Today Better

_____

_____

Notes

_____

_____

_____

_____

_____

_____

Date: _____

Today I Am Feeling:

_____

Today I Am Grateful For:

_____
_____
_____

Quote of the Day

3 Amazing Things That Happened Today

1. _____
2. _____
3. _____

My Happiness Scale Today:

Date: _____

The Best Part of My Day Was:
_____

This Person that Brought Me Joy Today
_____
_____

What Could I Have Done to Make Today Better
_____
_____

Notes
_____
_____
_____
_____
_____
_____
_____

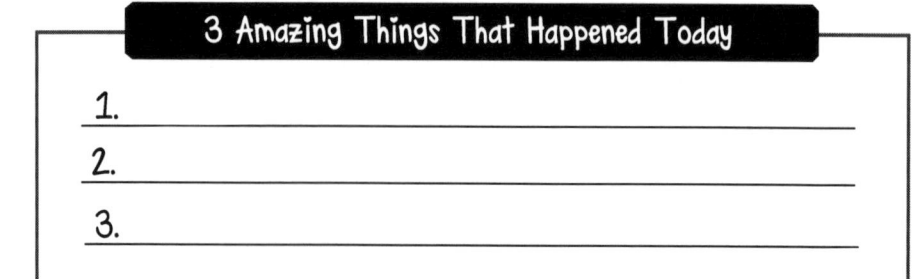

Date: _____

Today I Am Feeling:

_____

Today I Am Grateful For:

_____
_____
_____

Quote of the Day

3 Amazing Things That Happened Today

1. _____
2. _____
3. _____

My Happiness Scale Today:

Date: _____

The Best Part of My Day Was:

This Person that Brought Me Joy Today

What Could I Have Done to Make Today Better

Notes

TODAY -I am- THANKFUL

Date: _____

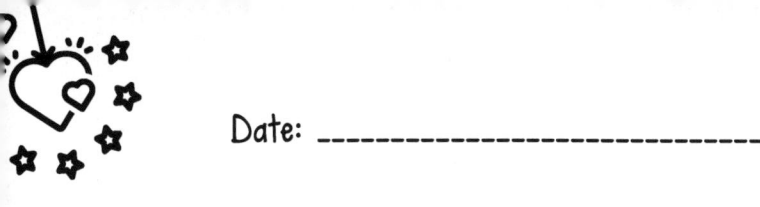

Today I Am Feeling:

_____

Today I Am Grateful For:

_____

_____

_____

Quote of the Day

3 Amazing Things That Happened Today

1. _____
2. _____
3. _____

My Happiness Scale Today:

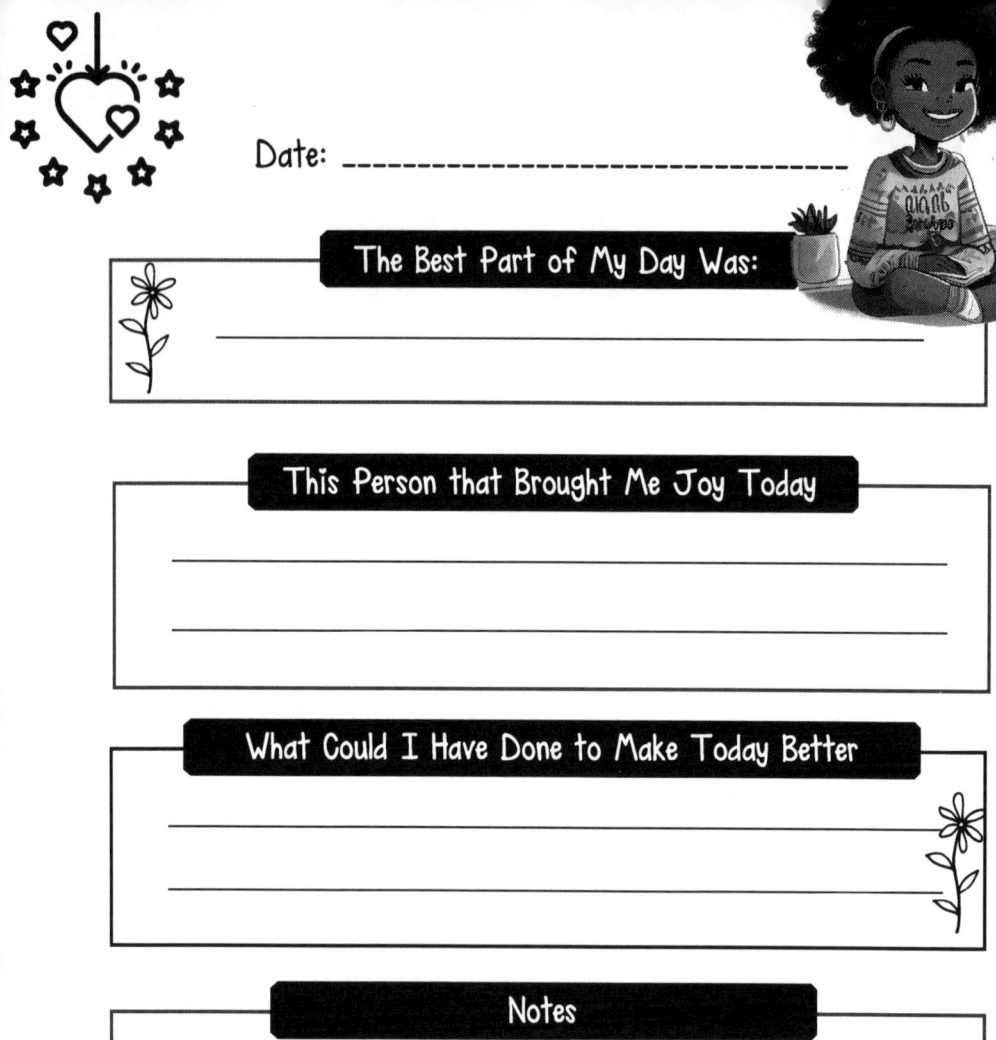

Date: _____

The Best Part of My Day Was:
_____
_____

This Person that Brought Me Joy Today
_____
_____

What Could I Have Done to Make Today Better
_____
_____

Notes
_____
_____
_____
_____
_____
_____

Date: _____

Today I Am Feeling:

_____

Today I Am Grateful For:

_____

_____

_____

Quote of the Day

3 Amazing Things That Happened Today

1. _____
2. _____
3. _____

My Happiness Scale Today:

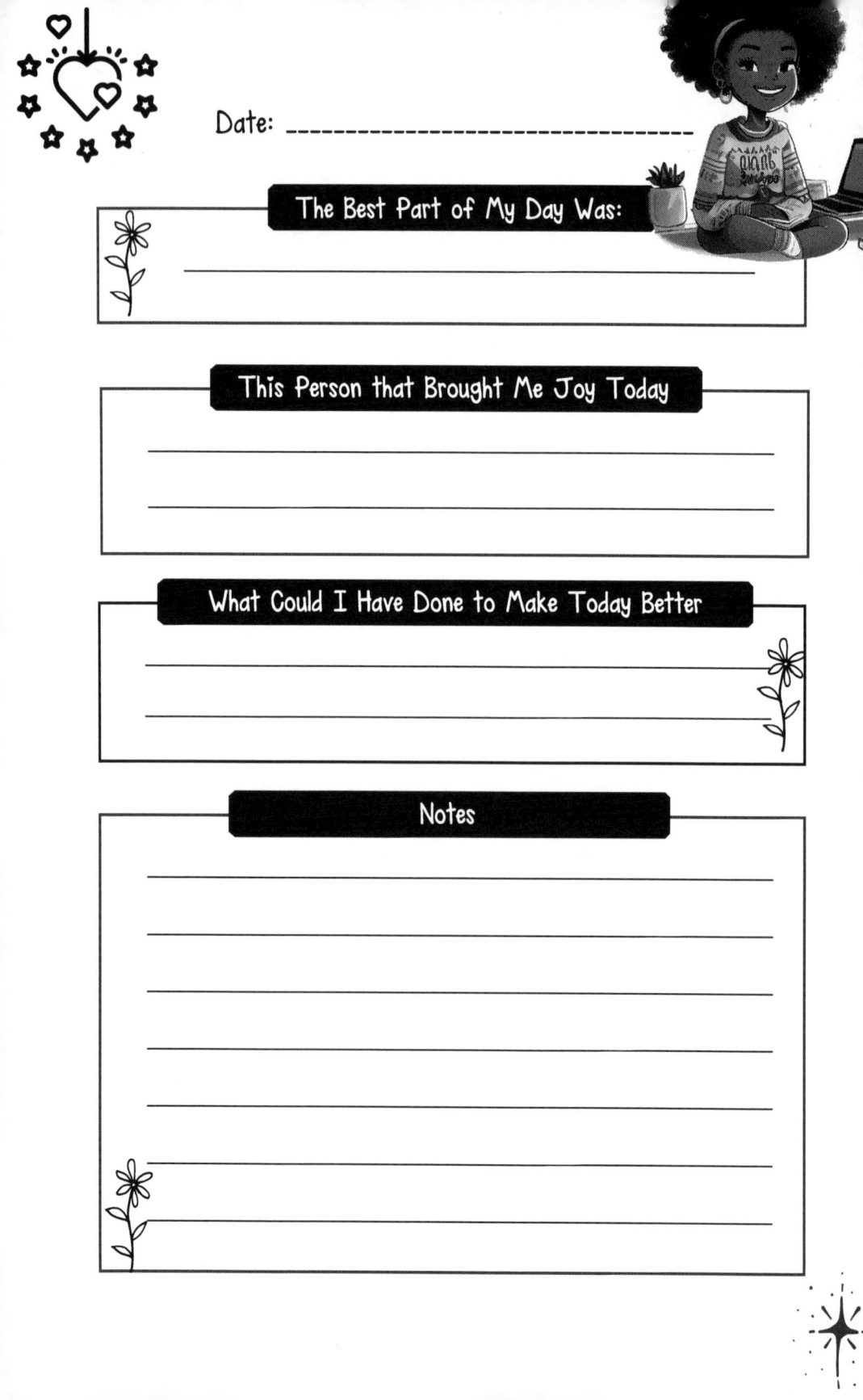

Date: _____

The Best Part of My Day Was:

This Person that Brought Me Joy Today

What Could I Have Done to Make Today Better

Notes

Date: _____

Today I Am Feeling:

_____

Today I Am Grateful For:

_____

_____

_____

Quote of the Day

3 Amazing Things That Happened Today

1. _____
2. _____
3. _____

My Happiness Scale Today:

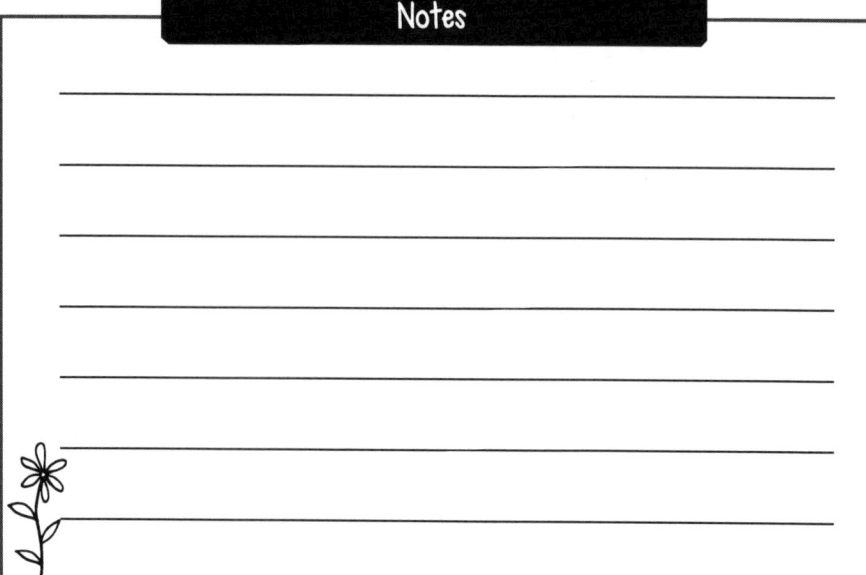

Date: _____

The Best Part of My Day Was:

This Person that Brought Me Joy Today

What Could I Have Done to Make Today Better

Notes

Date: _____

Today I Am Feeling:

_____

Today I Am Grateful For:

_____
_____
_____

Quote of the Day

3 Amazing Things That Happened Today

1. _____
2. _____
3. _____

My Happiness Scale Today:

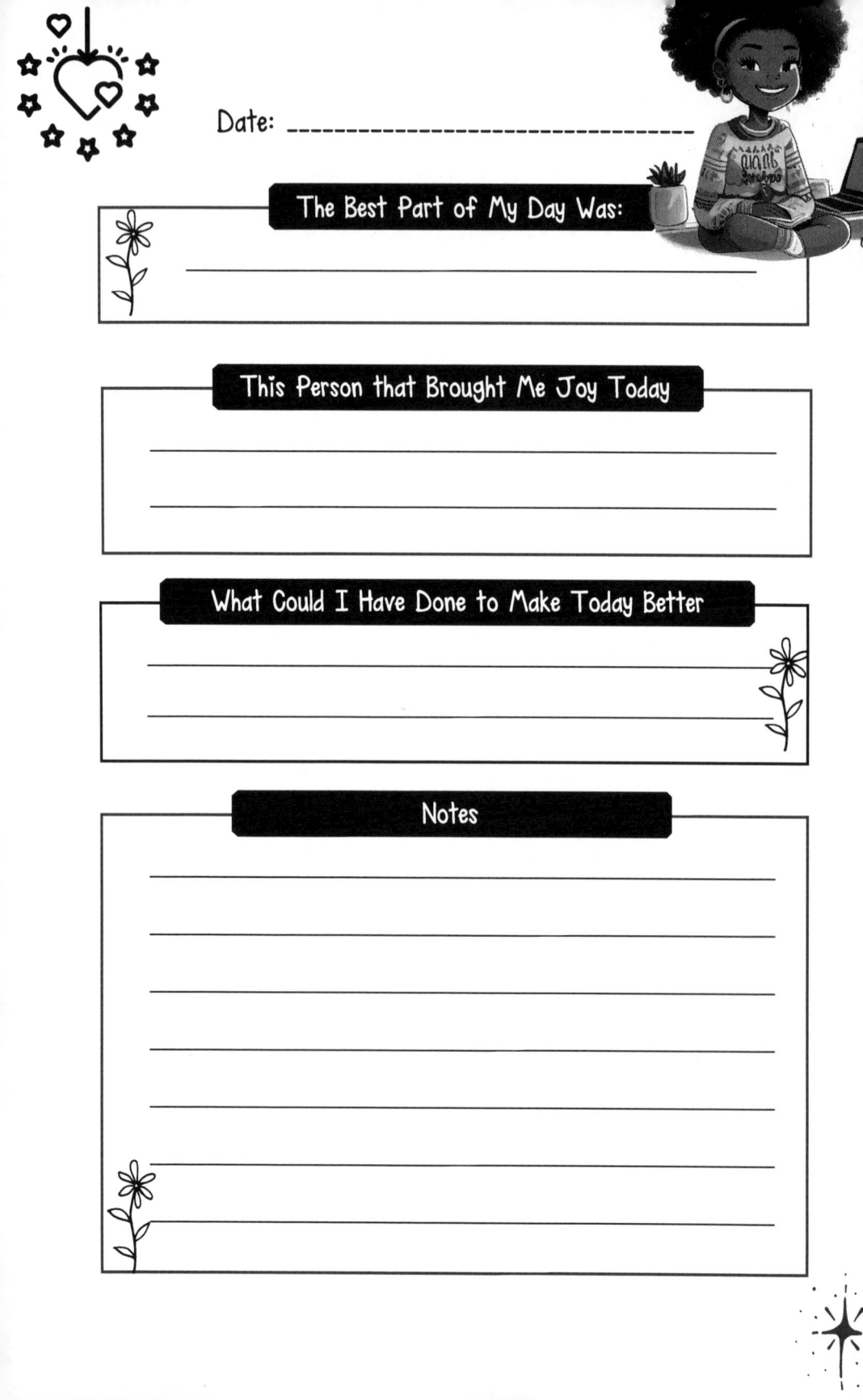

Date: _____

The Best Part of My Day Was:

This Person that Brought Me Joy Today

What Could I Have Done to Make Today Better

Notes

Date: _____

Today I Am Feeling:
_____

Today I Am Grateful For:
_____
_____
_____

Quote of the Day

3 Amazing Things That Happened Today
1. _____
2. _____
3. _____

My Happiness Scale Today:

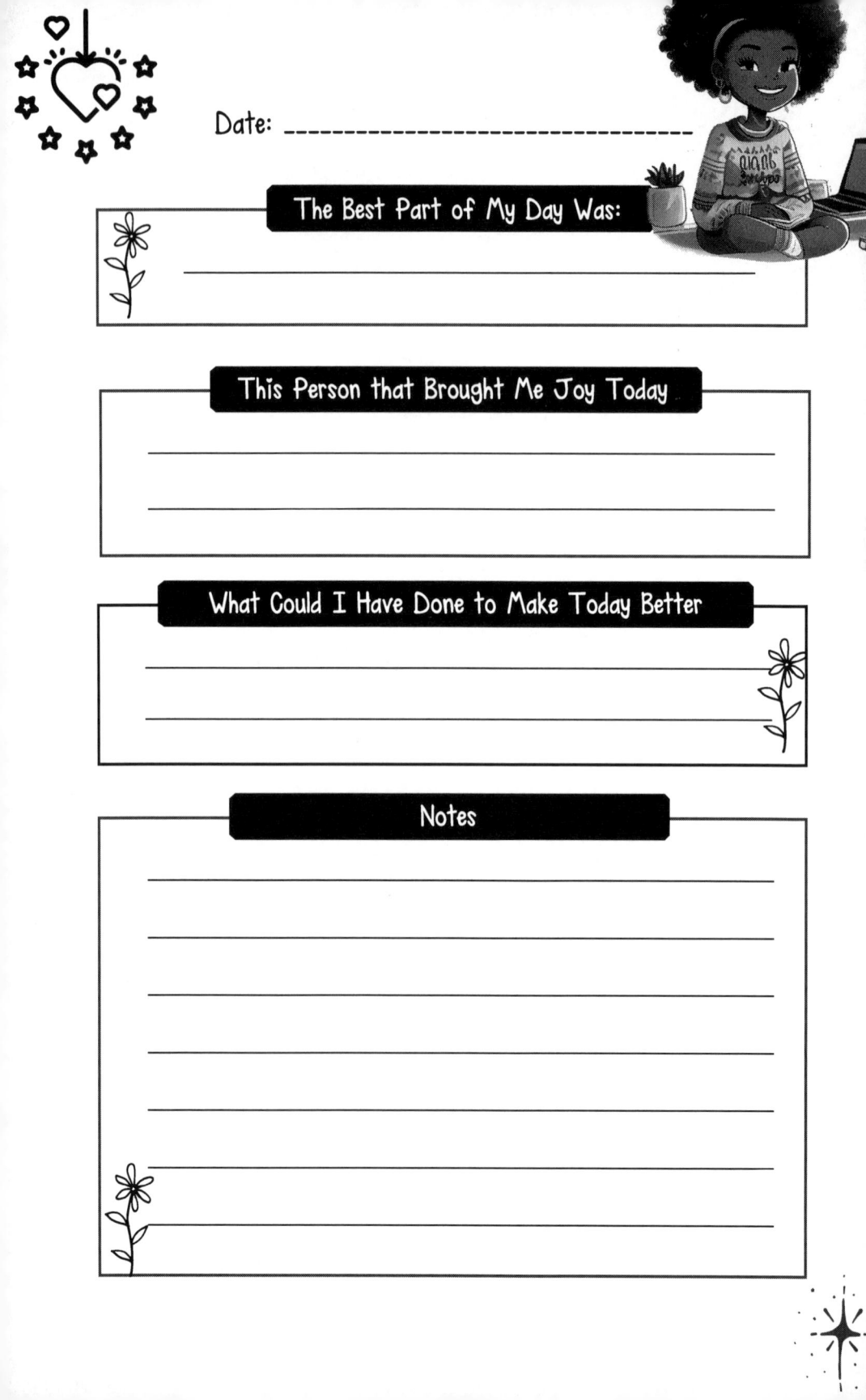

Date: _____

The Best Part of My Day Was:

This Person that Brought Me Joy Today

What Could I Have Done to Make Today Better

Notes

I AM SO GRATEFUL

Date: _____

Today I Am Feeling:

Today I Am Grateful For:

Quote of the Day

3 Amazing Things That Happened Today

1. _____
2. _____
3. _____

My Happiness Scale Today:

Date: _____

The Best Part of My Day Was:

_____

This Person that Brought Me Joy Today

_____

_____

What Could I Have Done to Make Today Better

_____

_____

Notes

_____

_____

_____

_____

_____

_____

Date: _____

Today I Am Feeling:

_____

Today I Am Grateful For:

_____
_____
_____

Quote of the Day

3 Amazing Things That Happened Today

1. _____
2. _____
3. _____

My Happiness Scale Today:

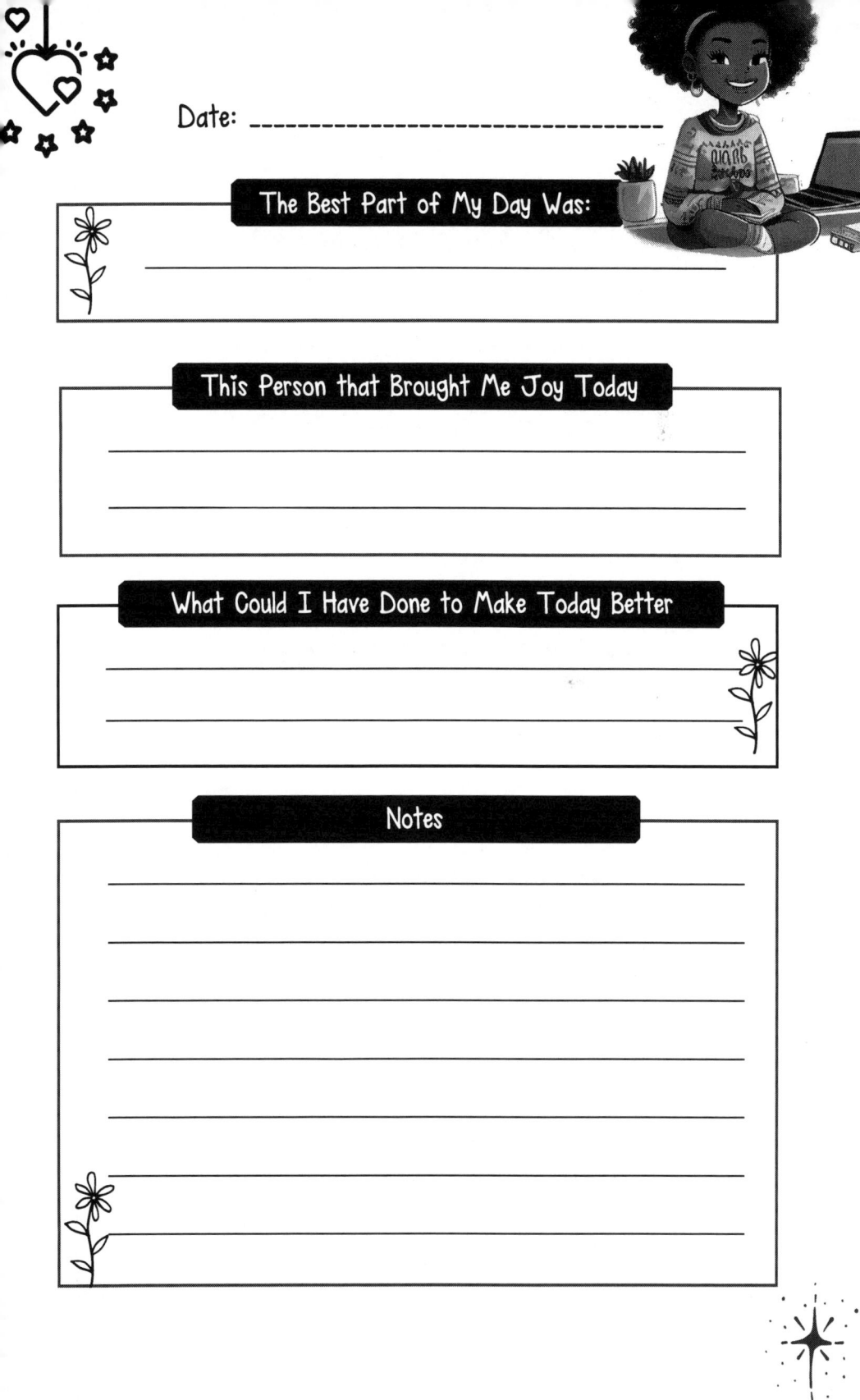

Date: _____

The Best Part of My Day Was:

_____

This Person that Brought Me Joy Today

_____

_____

What Could I Have Done to Make Today Better

_____

_____

Notes

_____

_____

_____

_____

_____

_____

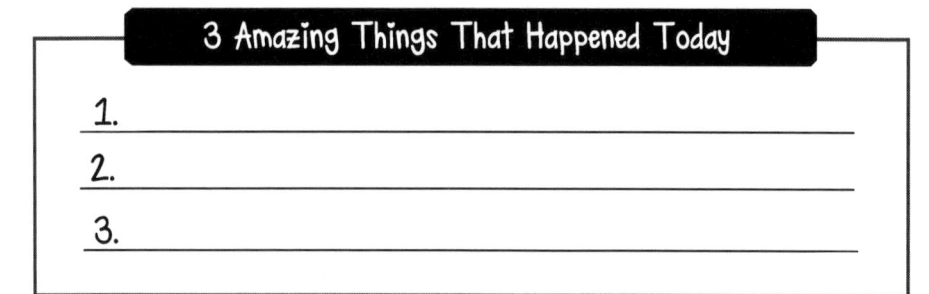

Date: _____

Today I Am Feeling:

_____

Today I Am Grateful For:

_____
_____
_____

Quote of the Day

3 Amazing Things That Happened Today

1. _____
2. _____
3. _____

My Happiness Scale Today:

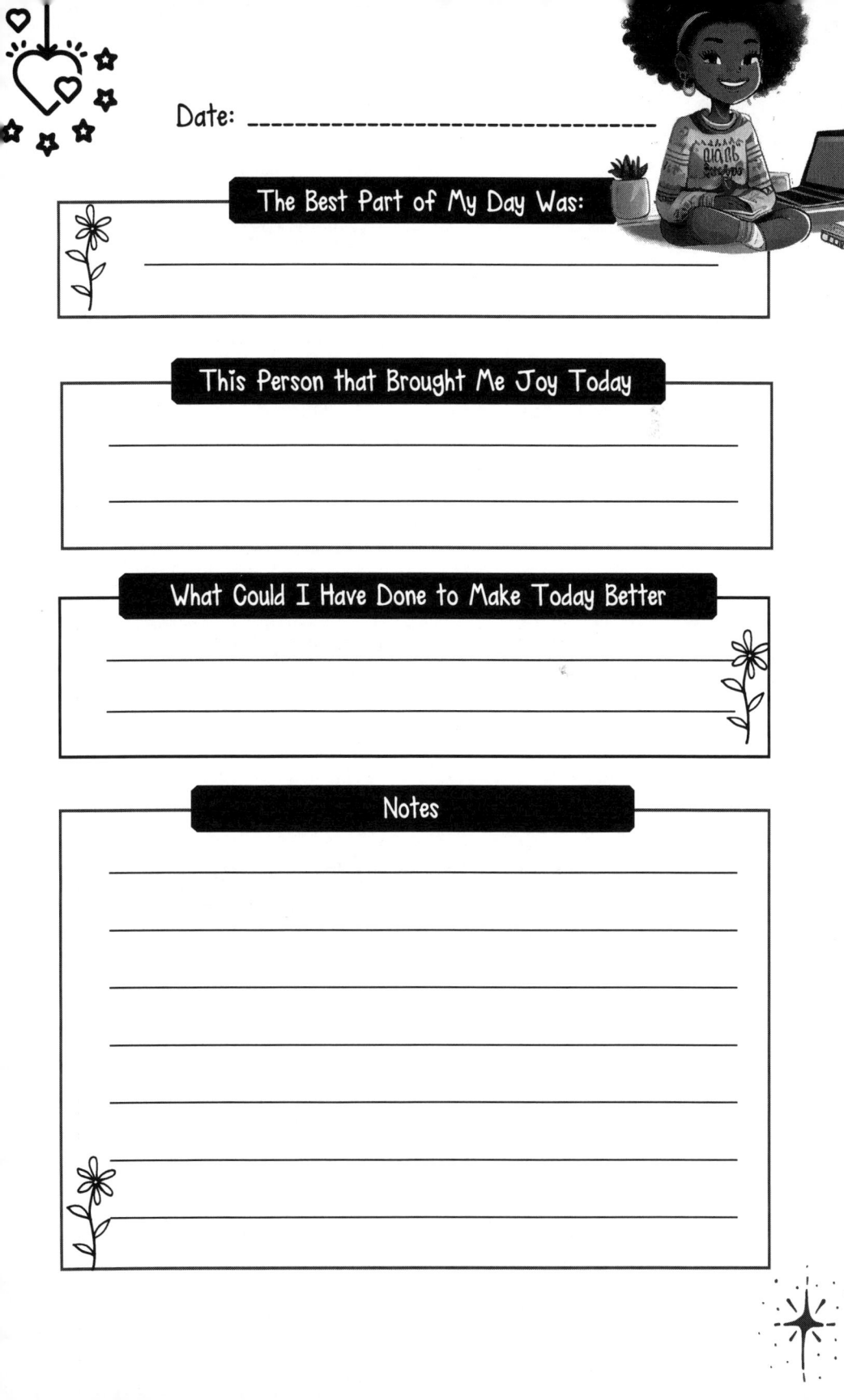

Date: _____

The Best Part of My Day Was:

_____

This Person that Brought Me Joy Today

_____
_____

What Could I Have Done to Make Today Better

_____
_____

Notes

_____
_____
_____
_____
_____
_____
_____

Date: _____

Today I Am Feeling:

_____

Today I Am Grateful For:

_____
_____
_____

Quote of the Day

3 Amazing Things That Happened Today

1. _____
2. _____
3. _____

My Happiness Scale Today:

Date: _____

The Best Part of My Day Was:

_____

This Person that Brought Me Joy Today

_____

_____

What Could I Have Done to Make Today Better

_____

_____

Notes

_____

_____

_____

_____

_____

_____

Date: _____

Today I Am Feeling:

_____

Today I Am Grateful For:

_____

_____

_____

Quote of the Day

3 Amazing Things That Happened Today

1. _____
2. _____
3. _____

My Happiness Scale Today:

Date: _____

The Best Part of My Day Was:
_____

This Person that Brought Me Joy Today
_____
_____

What Could I Have Done to Make Today Better
_____
_____

Notes
_____
_____
_____
_____
_____
_____
_____

nothing but gratitude!

Date: _____

Today I Am Feeling:

_____

Today I Am Grateful For:

_____
_____
_____

Quote of the Day

3 Amazing Things That Happened Today

1. _____
2. _____
3. _____

My Happiness Scale Today:

Date: _____

The Best Part of My Day Was:
_____

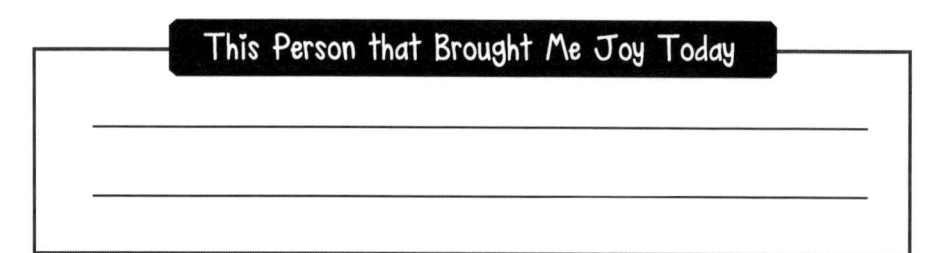

This Person that Brought Me Joy Today
_____
_____

What Could I Have Done to Make Today Better
_____
_____

Notes
_____
_____
_____
_____
_____
_____
_____

Date: _____

Today I Am Feeling:

Today I Am Grateful For:

Quote of the Day

3 Amazing Things That Happened Today

1.
2.
3.

My Happiness Scale Today:

Date: _____

The Best Part of My Day Was:
_____

This Person that Brought Me Joy Today
_____
_____

What Could I Have Done to Make Today Better
_____
_____

Notes
_____
_____
_____
_____
_____
_____
_____

Date: _____

Today I Am Feeling:

_____

Today I Am Grateful For:

_____

_____

_____

Quote of the Day

3 Amazing Things That Happened Today

1. _____
2. _____
3. _____

My Happiness Scale Today:

Date: _____

The Best Part of My Day Was:
_____

This Person that Brought Me Joy Today
_____
_____

What Could I Have Done to Make Today Better
_____
_____

Notes
_____
_____
_____
_____
_____
_____

Date: _____

Today I Am Feeling:

_____

Today I Am Grateful For:

_____

_____

_____

Quote of the Day

3 Amazing Things That Happened Today

1. _____
2. _____
3. _____

My Happiness Scale Today:

Date: _____

The Best Part of My Day Was:

_____

This Person that Brought Me Joy Today

_____

_____

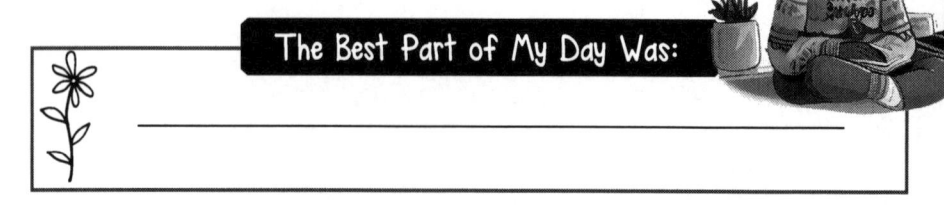

What Could I Have Done to Make Today Better

_____

_____

Notes

_____

_____

_____

_____

_____

_____

Date: _____

Today I Am Feeling:

_____

Today I Am Grateful For:

_____

_____

_____

Quote of the Day

3 Amazing Things That Happened Today

1. _____
2. _____
3. _____

My Happiness Scale Today:

Date: _____

The Best Part of My Day Was:

_____

This Person that Brought Me Joy Today

_____

_____

What Could I Have Done to Make Today Better

_____

_____

Notes

_____

_____

_____

_____

_____

_____

_____

give THANKS WITH A GRATEFUL heart

Date: _____

Today I Am Feeling:

_____

Today I Am Grateful For:

_____

_____

_____

Quote of the Day

3 Amazing Things That Happened Today

1. _____
2. _____
3. _____

My Happiness Scale Today:

Date: _____

The Best Part of My Day Was:
_____

This Person that Brought Me Joy Today
_____
_____

What Could I Have Done to Make Today Better
_____
_____

Notes
_____
_____
_____
_____
_____
_____
_____

Date: _____

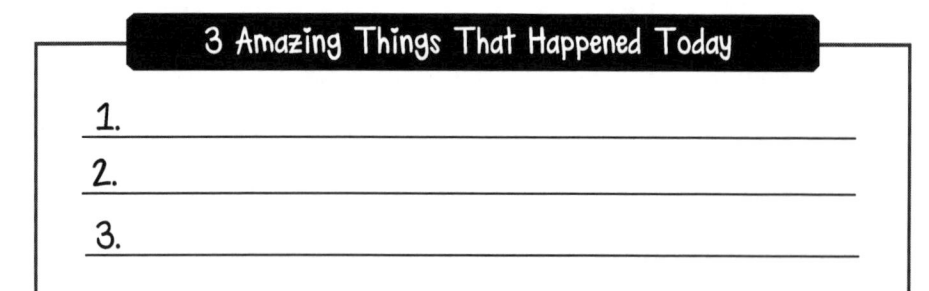

Today I Am Feeling:

_____

Today I Am Grateful For:

_____

_____

_____

Quote of the Day

3 Amazing Things That Happened Today

1. _____
2. _____
3. _____

My Happiness Scale Today:

Date: _____

The Best Part of My Day Was:

_____

This Person that Brought Me Joy Today

_____

_____

What Could I Have Done to Make Today Better

_____

_____

Notes

_____

_____

_____

_____

_____

_____

_____

Date: _____

Today I Am Feeling:

_____

Today I Am Grateful For:

_____

_____

_____

Quote of the Day

3 Amazing Things That Happened Today

1. _____
2. _____
3. _____

My Happiness Scale Today:

Date: _____

The Best Part of My Day Was:

_____

This Person that Brought Me Joy Today

_____
_____

What Could I Have Done to Make Today Better

_____
_____

Notes

_____
_____
_____
_____
_____
_____
_____

Date: _____

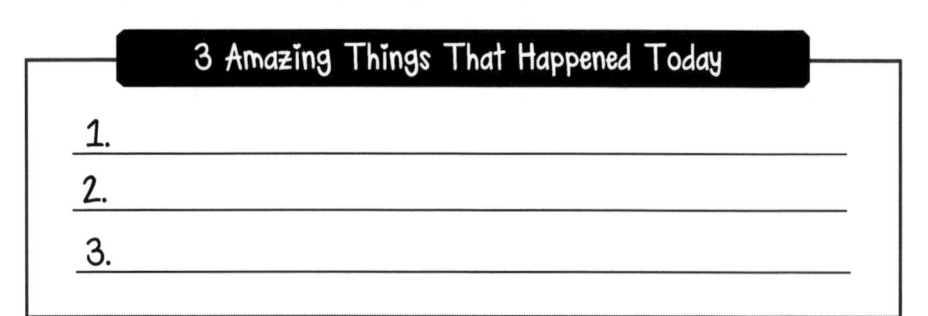

Today I Am Feeling:

_____

Today I Am Grateful For:

_____

_____

_____

Quote of the Day

3 Amazing Things That Happened Today

1. _____
2. _____
3. _____

My Happiness Scale Today:

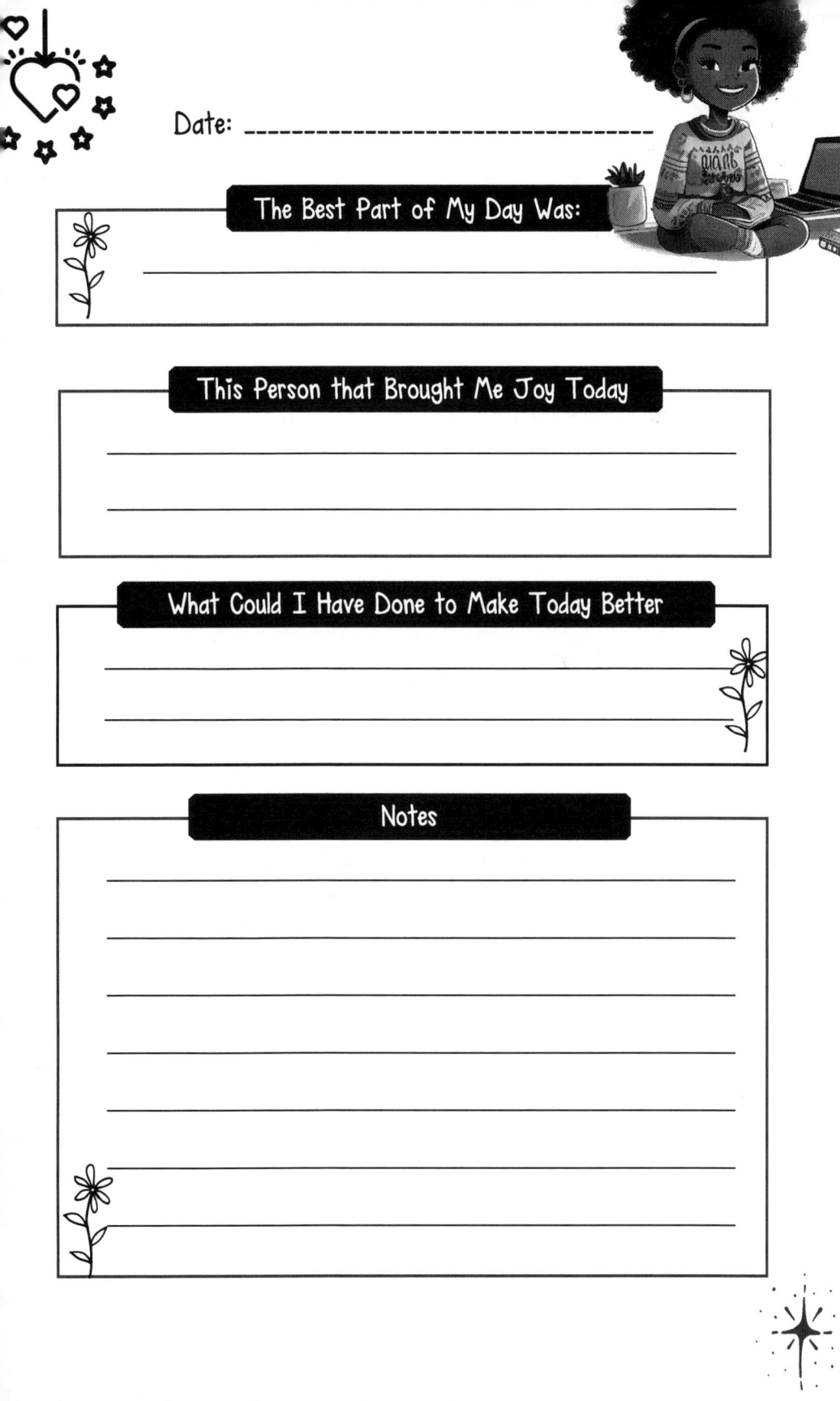

Date: _____

The Best Part of My Day Was:

_____

This Person that Brought Me Joy Today

_____
_____

What Could I Have Done to Make Today Better

_____
_____

Notes

_____
_____
_____
_____
_____
_____
_____

Date: _____

Today I Am Feeling:

_____

Today I Am Grateful For:

_____
_____
_____

Quote of the Day

3 Amazing Things That Happened Today

1. _____
2. _____
3. _____

My Happiness Scale Today:

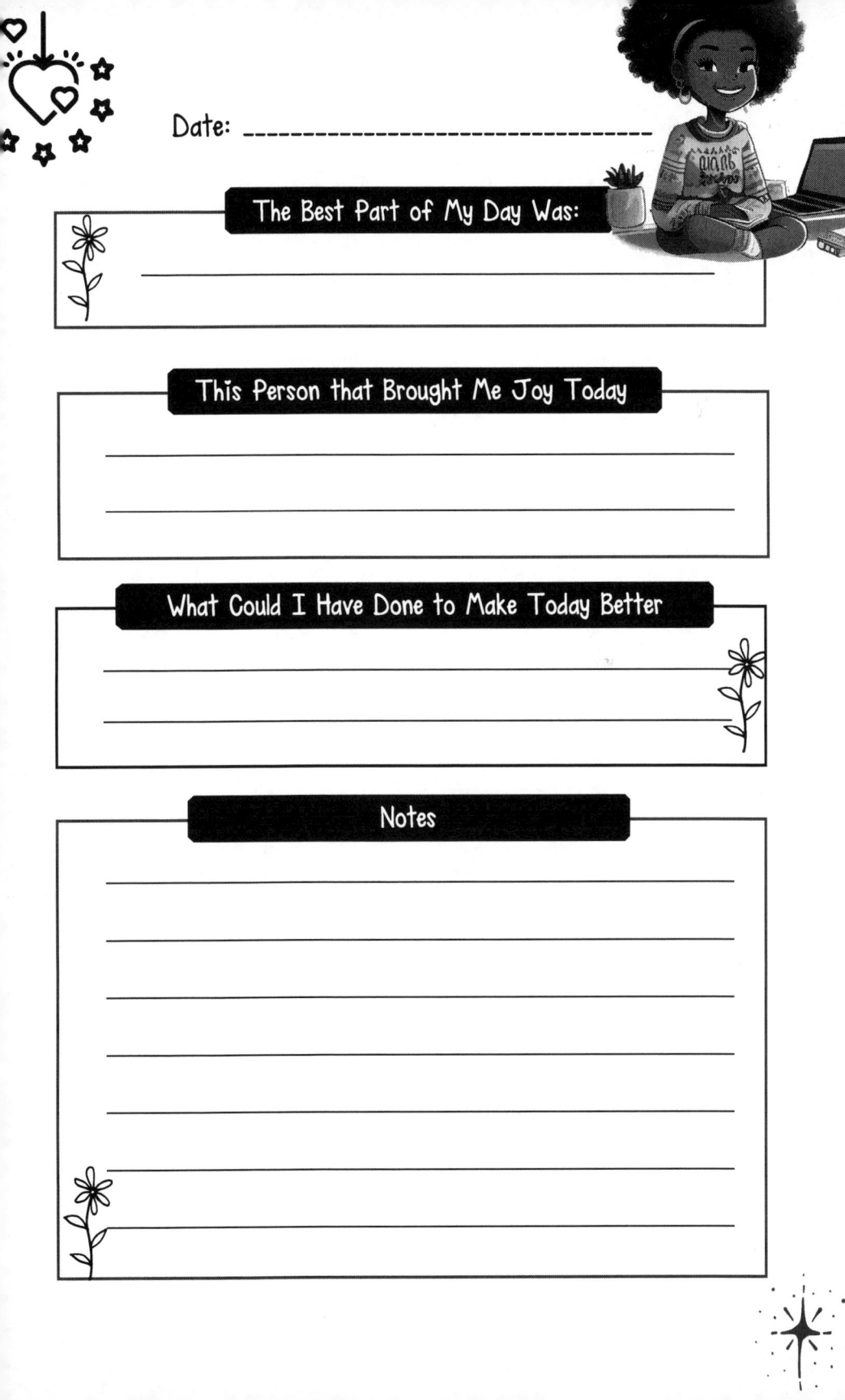

Date: _____

The Best Part of My Day Was:

_____
_____

This Person that Brought Me Joy Today

_____
_____

What Could I Have Done to Make Today Better

_____
_____

Notes

_____
_____
_____
_____
_____
_____
_____

Date: _____

Today I Am Feeling:

_____

Today I Am Grateful For:

_____

_____

_____

Quote of the Day

3 Amazing Things That Happened Today

1. _____
2. _____
3. _____

My Happiness Scale Today:

Date: _____

The Best Part of My Day Was:

_____

This Person that Brought Me Joy Today

_____

_____

What Could I Have Done to Make Today Better

_____

_____

Notes

_____

_____

_____

_____

_____

_____

Date: _____

Today I Am Feeling:

_____

Today I Am Grateful For:

_____

_____

_____

Quote of the Day

3 Amazing Things That Happened Today

1. _____
2. _____
3. _____

My Happiness Scale Today:

Date: _____

The Best Part of My Day Was:

This Person that Brought Me Joy Today

What Could I Have Done to Make Today Better

Notes

Date: _____

Today I Am Feeling:
_____

Today I Am Grateful For:
_____
_____
_____

Quote of the Day

3 Amazing Things That Happened Today
1. _____
2. _____
3. _____

My Happiness Scale Today:

Date: _____

The Best Part of My Day Was:

This Person that Brought Me Joy Today

What Could I Have Done to Make Today Better

Notes

Date: _____

Today I Am Feeling:

_____

Today I Am Grateful For:

_____

_____

_____

Quote of the Day

3 Amazing Things That Happened Today

1. _____
2. _____
3. _____

My Happiness Scale Today:

Date: _____

The Best Part of My Day Was:
_____

This Person that Brought Me Joy Today
_____
_____

What Could I Have Done to Make Today Better
_____
_____

Notes
_____
_____
_____
_____
_____
_____
_____

Date: _____

Today I Am Feeling:

_____

Today I Am Grateful For:

_____

_____

_____

Quote of the Day

3 Amazing Things That Happened Today

1. _____
2. _____
3. _____

My Happiness Scale Today:

Date: _____

The Best Part of My Day Was:

_____

This Person that Brought Me Joy Today

_____

_____

What Could I Have Done to Make Today Better

_____

_____

Notes

_____

_____

_____

_____

_____

_____

SO VERY
thankful
INCREDIBLY
grateful
UNBELIEVABLY
blessed

Date: _____

Today I Am Feeling:

_____

Today I Am Grateful For:

_____

_____

_____

Quote of the Day

3 Amazing Things That Happened Today

1. _____
2. _____
3. _____

My Happiness Scale Today:

Date: _____

The Best Part of My Day Was:

_____

This Person that Brought Me Joy Today

_____

_____

What Could I Have Done to Make Today Better

_____

_____

Notes

_____

_____

_____

_____

_____

_____

_____

Date: _____

Today I Am Feeling:

_____

Today I Am Grateful For:

_____

_____

_____

Quote of the Day

3 Amazing Things That Happened Today

1. _____
2. _____
3. _____

My Happiness Scale Today:

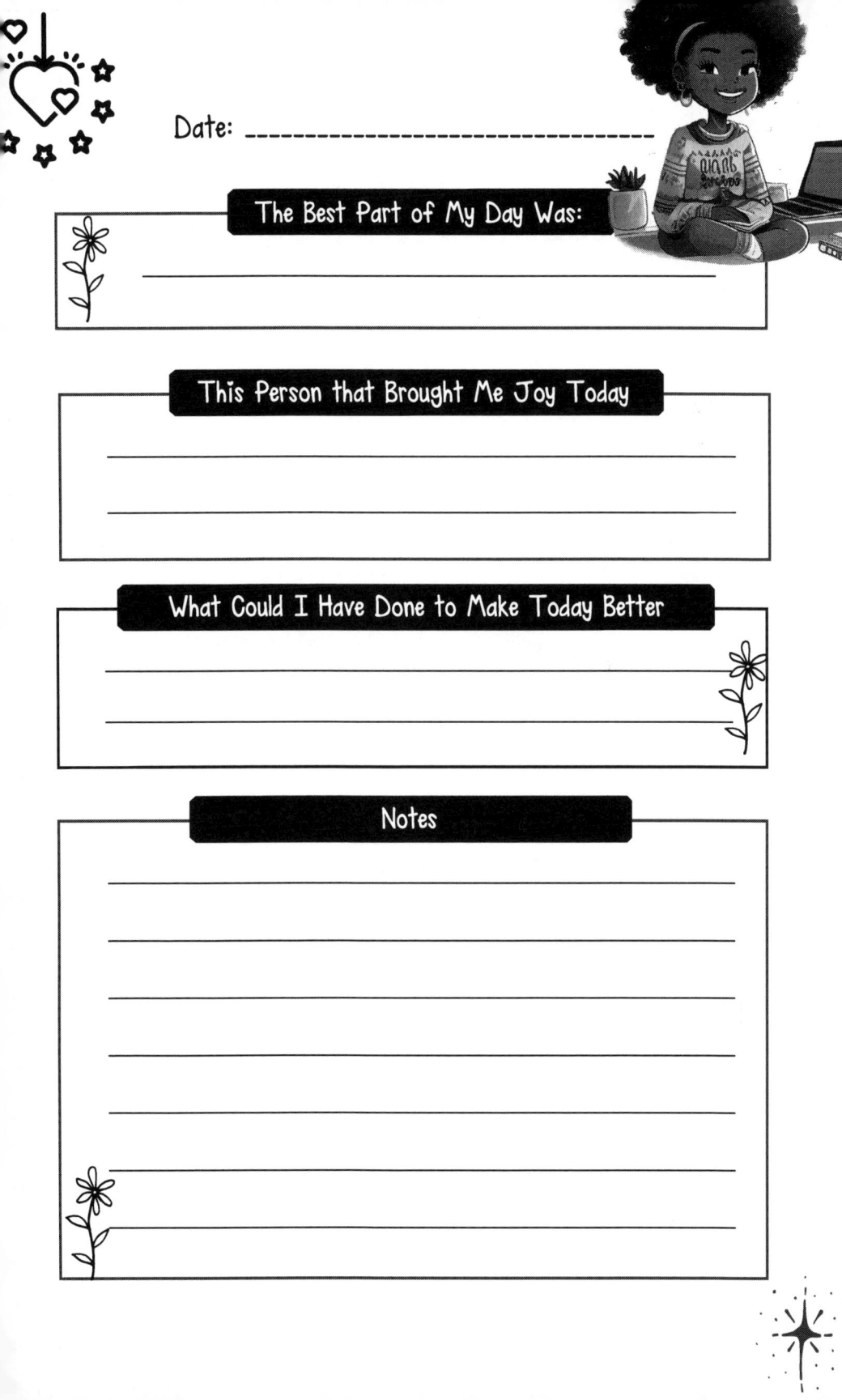

Date: _____

The Best Part of My Day Was:

This Person that Brought Me Joy Today

What Could I Have Done to Make Today Better

Notes

Date: _____

Today I Am Feeling:

_____

Today I Am Grateful For:

_____

_____

_____

Quote of the Day

3 Amazing Things That Happened Today

1. _____
2. _____
3. _____

My Happiness Scale Today:

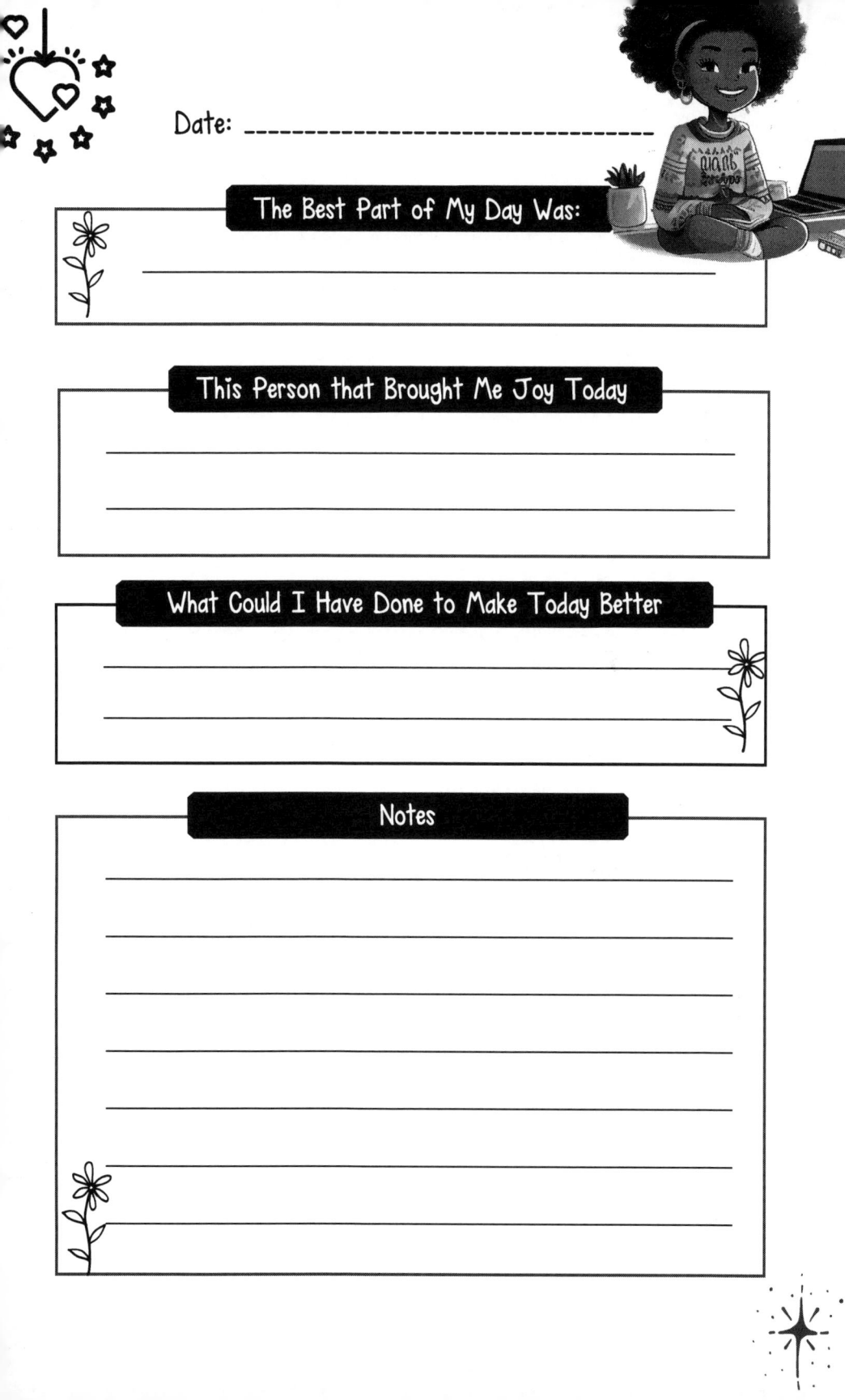

Date: _____

The Best Part of My Day Was:

This Person that Brought Me Joy Today

What Could I Have Done to Make Today Better

Notes

Date: _____

Today I Am Feeling:

_____

Today I Am Grateful For:

_____

_____

_____

Quote of the Day

3 Amazing Things That Happened Today

1. _____
2. _____
3. _____

My Happiness Scale Today:

Date: _____

The Best Part of My Day Was:
_____
_____

This Person that Brought Me Joy Today
_____
_____

What Could I Have Done to Make Today Better
_____
_____

Notes
_____
_____
_____
_____
_____
_____
_____

Date: _____

Today I Am Feeling:

_____

Today I Am Grateful For:

_____

_____

_____

Quote of the Day

3 Amazing Things That Happened Today

1. _____
2. _____
3. _____

My Happiness Scale Today:

Date: _____

The Best Part of My Day Was:

_____

This Person that Brought Me Joy Today

_____
_____

What Could I Have Done to Make Today Better

_____
_____

Notes

_____
_____
_____
_____
_____
_____
_____

BLESSED

Date: _____

Today I Am Feeling:

_____

Today I Am Grateful For:

_____
_____
_____

Quote of the Day

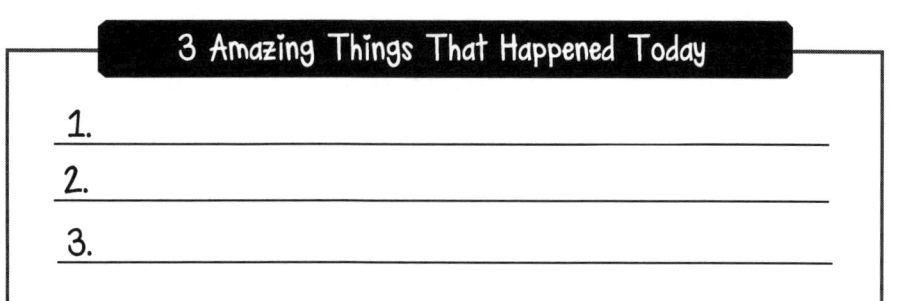

3 Amazing Things That Happened Today

1. _____
2. _____
3. _____

My Happiness Scale Today:

Date: _____

The Best Part of My Day Was:
_____

This Person that Brought Me Joy Today
_____
_____

What Could I Have Done to Make Today Better
_____
_____

Notes
_____
_____
_____
_____
_____
_____

Date: _____

Today I Am Feeling:
_____

Today I Am Grateful For:
_____
_____
_____

Quote of the Day

3 Amazing Things That Happened Today
1. _____
2. _____
3. _____

My Happiness Scale Today:

Date: _____

The Best Part of My Day Was:

_____

This Person that Brought Me Joy Today

_____
_____

What Could I Have Done to Make Today Better

_____
_____

Notes

_____
_____
_____
_____
_____
_____

Date: _____

Today I Am Feeling:
_____

Today I Am Grateful For:
_____
_____
_____

Quote of the Day

3 Amazing Things That Happened Today
1. _____
2. _____
3. _____

My Happiness Scale Today:

Date: _____

The Best Part of My Day Was:

_____

This Person that Brought Me Joy Today

_____

_____

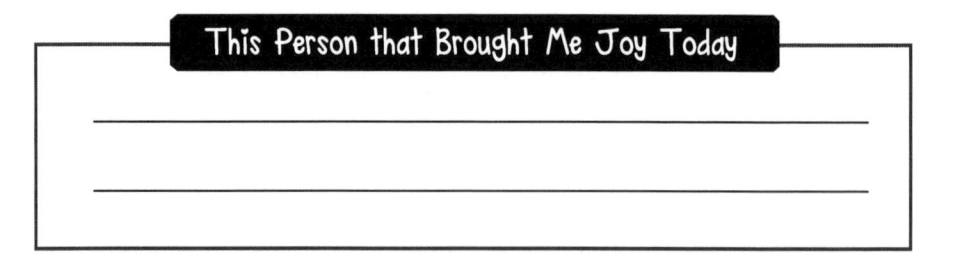

What Could I Have Done to Make Today Better

_____

_____

Notes

_____

_____

_____

_____

_____

_____

Date: _____

Today I Am Feeling:
_____

Today I Am Grateful For:
_____
_____
_____

Quote of the Day

3 Amazing Things That Happened Today
1. _____
2. _____
3. _____

My Happiness Scale Today:

Date: _____

The Best Part of My Day Was:

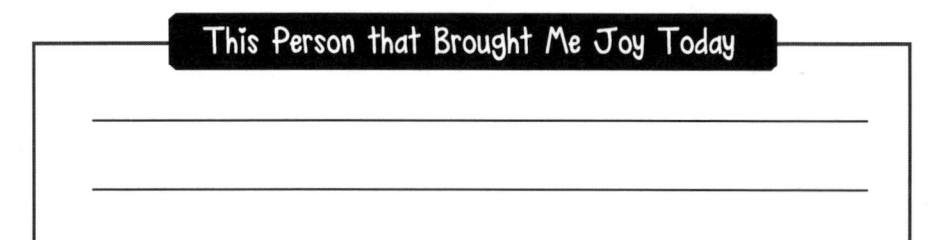

_____

This Person that Brought Me Joy Today

_____

_____

What Could I Have Done to Make Today Better

_____

_____

Notes

_____

_____

_____

_____

_____

_____

Date: _____

Today I Am Feeling:

_____

Today I Am Grateful For:

_____

_____

_____

Quote of the Day

3 Amazing Things That Happened Today

1. _____
2. _____
3. _____

My Happiness Scale Today:

Date: _____

The Best Part of My Day Was:

_____

This Person that Brought Me Joy Today

_____
_____

What Could I Have Done to Make Today Better

_____
_____

Notes

_____
_____
_____
_____
_____
_____

BLESSED

Date: _____

Today I Am Feeling:

_____

Today I Am Grateful For:

_____
_____
_____

Quote of the Day

3 Amazing Things That Happened Today

1. _____
2. _____
3. _____

My Happiness Scale Today:

Date: _____

The Best Part of My Day Was:

_____

This Person that Brought Me Joy Today

_____

_____

What Could I Have Done to Make Today Better

_____

_____

Notes

_____

_____

_____

_____

_____

_____

Date: _____

Today I Am Feeling:

_____

Today I Am Grateful For:

_____

_____

_____

Quote of the Day

3 Amazing Things That Happened Today

1. _____
2. _____
3. _____

My Happiness Scale Today:

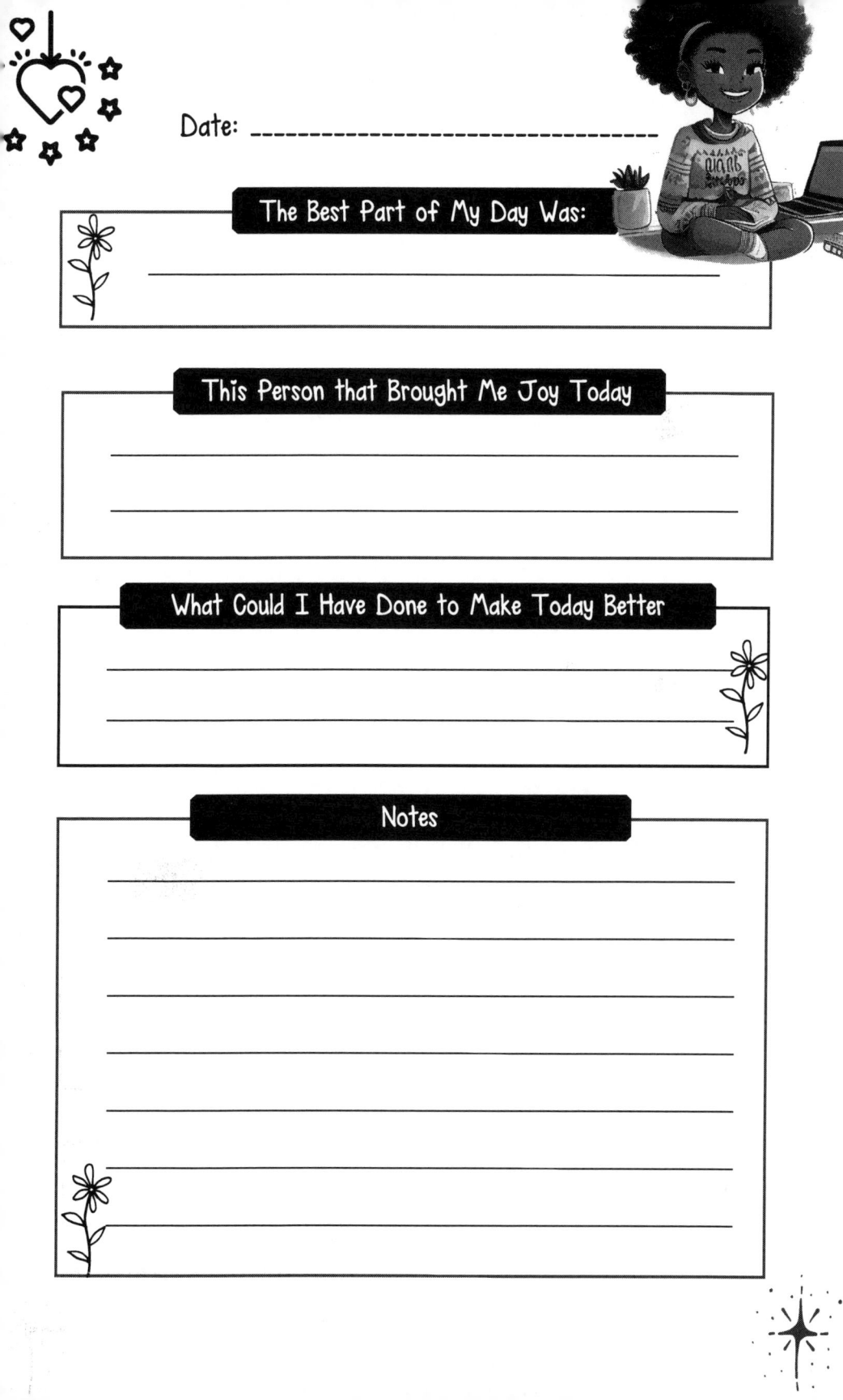

Date: _____

The Best Part of My Day Was:

_____

This Person that Brought Me Joy Today

_____

_____

What Could I Have Done to Make Today Better

_____

_____

Notes

_____

_____

_____

_____

_____

_____

Printed in Great Britain
by Amazon